# Little dark truths:

## *A Collection of Poems*

**Kiersten Anderson**

*I dedicate this book to my loving husband Derek and our two wild beasts Bogart and Maybelline.*

*To the reader:*

*Little Dark Truths was an incredible writing experience for me, I dug deep into my thoughts, dreams and things that make my heart ache. Some of the topics I've chosen to write about may not be favorable among many, but they are truth, nonetheless. These poems came straight from the heart of what I feel, and life experience. Poetry is an emotional experience and a fantastic way to showcase creativity.*

*I hope you enjoy.*

*Kiersten Anderson*

*Poet*

*I've gone most of my life only telling my deepest thoughts to a piece of paper.*

*-Kiersten Anderson*

<u>Stones</u>

*With stones in her pockets*

*She lies on the shore*

*As each wave overcomes her*

*She ponders memories galore*


*She'd hoped someone would save her from herself*

*But no one was left*

*Her life was just a story on a shelf*


*Her body flowed with the current*

*And sank with the weight*

*Of life's heavy burdens*

*And the whiskey she drank*


*Voices heard overhead*

*And the sound of a motor*

*Was she dead?*


*Splashes ensued and arms were grasped*

*Did someone care about her?*


*A second chance was here at last*

<u>Little Lambs</u>

*Little lambs so innocent,*

*So pure.*

*Led to the slaughter*

*For what*

*They're unsure.*


*To remove their meat,*

*And leave the bones*

*As if no life was taken from its home.*

<u>**Morbid Dance**</u>

*Darkness comes with pain when the doctors say there's little chance.*

*The worry in my brain won't stop its morbid dance.*

*Terror and fright haunt me in the night.*

*I dwell in their delight.*

<u>Brick and Mortar</u>

*Void of all emotions it seems.*

*Do you feel a thing for me?*

*I try, I try*

*I pry, I pry*

*The mortar and brick build up so high*

*A wall too high for me to climb.*

<u>**Woes**</u>

*I open my eyes to live the day.*

*When could I close my eyes to live on in slumber?*

*Preserving my heart and mind from the woes the day would bring.*

<u>Sweet Birds</u>

*The darkness is gone*

*The sweet bird sings outside my window*

*My fear disappears with each melodic note*

*The suns early arrival casts an invitation to all*

*To forget the night*

*Forget your fears*

*Take the day as your own*

<u>Lost you</u>

*Some days have passed since the world lost you.*

*My appetite has returned,*

*Most crying has ceased,*

*But my heart still grieves you.*

*Somehow, it's gotten easier to accept you're gone,*

*And for that I feel guilt.*

*Praying your ghost visits me is the only hope I feel.*

## <u>Death Flowers</u>

*Bought on a Sunday to brighten your room.*

*They sat in a corner by the window,*

*Beautiful blooms.*

*I'd hoped they'd brighten your days,*

*But on that Thursday the nurses would say that you left peacefully.*

*You stole a part of me.*

*We said our good-bye's,*

*We felt our deep, piercing cries.*

*Our hearts hold every moment,*

*And our souls are tied.*


*Now those hospital blooms,*

*Present for your last breath,*

*Sit among me in my room.*

*Un-aged.*

*Un-touched.*

<u>**Hope**</u>

*I hope you're on the water holding the moon in your hands.*

*Feeling our love from within,*

*And the earth shaking the sands.*


*I hope you feel at ease,*

*As though you've had a timely slumber,*

*And I hope you remember me and keep me safe from the thunder.*


*I hope your eyes are lit with a heavenly glaze,*

*And that you come to find me one of these days.*


*I hope your body feels a new,*

*I hope your mind feels it too.*

<u>Opportunity</u>

*My shoes traipsing through fallen limbs and leaves of grass,*

*so green and slick.*

*Air fills my lungs; I feel a change. change among me and the trees*

*newness of life,*

*rebirth.*

*breezes of opportunity,*

*Rays of hope shining on me*

*songbirds chanting their love*

*for life through the trees*

*the trees silently whispering to the Sky*

*the sun cascading its wisdom to me alone.*

_<u>Before Him</u>_

*I'd follow you into the darkness,*

*Upon the burning sand.*

*I'll stand with you before the devil,*

*And we'll exchange our bands.*

*For the love that burns so purely,*

*And with the flames we did dance.*

*Hold my hand forever,*

*My sweet beloved man.*

## The Black woods

*My feet cut from the ground beneath.*

*Dodging every tree that grazes me.*

*Black are the woods.*

*Frigid is the night.*

*Naked is my body,*

*As I follow sounds of midnight.*

*My eyes are blinded with black,*

*Now,*

*Nothing but memories can get me back.*

<u>*Crimson*</u>

*Your crimson words cut me to my marrow.*

*Your presence makes me hollow.*

*The know it all existence that you carry*

*Is resistance to the ignorance you bury.*

<u>Weak</u>


*Her face whitened with his stare.*

*Her heartbeat grew faster; he knew she was scared.*

*Her eyes fluttered to find an escape.*

*But the room was a circle; her vulnerability left agape.*

*He took advantage of her weak body and lost soul.*

*She never left that room completely whole.*

<u>*She*</u>

*With secret pockets hidden to hide,*

*Nothing but her soul inside.*


*She opens her heart as a guide, to take a journey*

*To the other side.*


*So, she could be more than someone's bride.*


*She watches the girls that giggle with glee,*

*For a man arriving from across the sea.*


*They fell for a falsity.*

*When they believed they were finally free.*

<u>You</u>

*I love the sound your heart makes as you breath in and out.*

*It reminds me of your existence,*

*Something my feeble soul couldn't live without.*


*You and me*

*Me and you*

*A passion nothing could ever break*

*Not even the hardships that make our tiny, brittle bones ache.*

<u>*Lost Soul*</u>

*He stalks the corner as I go to sleep.*

*As soon as my eyes shut,*

*I hear his feet.*

*His looming presence hovers over me.*

*My body, afraid to move.*

*To breath.*

*He stands there for hours.*

*Examining me with his hollow black eyes.*

*His presence still haunts me.*

*His motive unsure.*

*Maybe I'll ask next time he returns.*

<u>*Into the night*</u>

*He told me to follow him into the night,*

*So, I put on my shoes and turned out the light.*

*We walked to a graveyard that I'd never seen.*

*He pointed to a headstone made for me.*

*The date was marked twenty years to this day.*

*How could I prevent this?*

*How could I make this go away?*

*With his boney fingers he grasped my face*

*"My Dear, don't you want to know how you got to this place?"*


*You'd follow a stranger into the night, without any notice, without any sight.*

*He'll lead you into the dark abyss,*

*And with one kiss,*

*You'll end up like this.*

<u>**Addiction**</u>

*My body lie cold and stiff*

*metal against my bones*

*numbness in my fingertips with nothing left to hold*

*my eyelids stuck with lashes matted*

*my brain felt black, thoughts of nothing emphatic*

*my breath feels captured in a bottle*

*my life lay still as I wait for an Apostle*

*I fear my funeral comes next*

*with much detail I can assume*

*to make it seem like my life was great and I never felt impending doom*

*with one needle I ended it all*

*I never thought of my family*

*I didn't think at all*

*if only I had one thought*

*one moment of grace*

*I'd go back and think about your face*

*It made my world a much better place*

<u>Tiny Girl</u>

*Tiny Girl inside my heart wants nothing but to please you*

*She holds a heroic picture of you*

*She ne'er forgets to tell you every detail of her life*

*Because she sincerely hopes you'll take delight*


*She searches for pride in you*

*She searches for a hand to hold*

*She can't withstand the cold*


*Oh, Tiny girl!*

*Can't you see that you are much too old for this fantasy?*

<u>**Under the Lilacs**</u>

*Under the lilacs in the garden she grew, also grew a secret she buried because of you.*

*Everyone wondered how she got them so blue.*

*Her secret: the man she loved, you murdered and cut into.*


*The moment you met him your jealousy ensued.*

*When he noticed the charm, you wore on your arm and the way she looked with you.*

*You noticed the way he stared at her.*

*You saw him tousle her hair.*

*You knew it was the start of a gruesome love affair.*


*You stopped by his house and saw them both there,*

*Lying in his bed with their clothes draped over the corner chair.*


*Your fists took over the air, eyes only saw red as you pinned him down by his neck in what was now a bloody bed.*


*She screamed, she wailed, "What did you do?"*

*The man's body was lifeless and beaten blue.*

*With screaming and crying blood down her cheeks, she helped you, a criminal, roll her man into a sheet.*

*With a battered heart she spoke, "I loved you both, but now you see I can't still love you when you took him away from me."*


*With a stroke of your hair she pulled out a gun and ended you beyond repair.*

<u>Traits</u>


*Rudeness must be your family trait*

*To just say whatever comes to mind*

*No matter the heart at stake*


*Loud mouths and shallow souls*

*are all you have to give.*


*So, take your empty words and obsolete opinions,*

*I have a life to live.*

<u>**Sea of forgetfulness**</u>



*In the sea of forgetfulness, I still remember.*

*Salt water in my wounds*

*I'm left to surrender*

*To the black seas of my memories of our time together.*

<u>The Psychic</u>

*With my palm face up on her satin tablecloth*

*She reads the wisdom that silently lies in the lines of my hand.*


*Closing her eyes, she takes a deep breath*

*Before she spills how my future will come to an end.*

**<u>They/We</u>**

*They grope,*

*They stare.*

*They tell you how to style your hair.*


*They depend on us for an heir to their misogynistic chair.*


*They hold you down,*

*And rip you up,*

*As your womanhood evaporates into thin air.*


*They expect us to stay in the kitchen,*

*To roast their chicken.*

*And to keep a neat house to raise their kids in.*


*They look down our blouse and think we can't see them*


*All we want is respect, and an equal world to live in.*

<u>**Poison**</u>

*Terrified I'm going to lose you to the poison you subject yourself to.*

*Every chance you get, you need a hit.*

*I don't want to get that call that you were found with no heartbeat at all*

*It terrifies me to think of your life without a shell*

*I never want to live that turmoil.*

*That's pure hell.*

<u>**My heart**</u>

*I've not lost every ounce of compassion.*

*But my heart is empty for betrayers,*

*Liars and slayers.*


*My heart is lost for those without sympathy for the weaker most innocent beings.*

<u>**Mama Said**</u>

*Mama said, "You can't save the whole world, honey."*

*She knew this.*

*But her compassion still wailed and wept.*


*Fear of what she had no control over*

*Felt like lives slipping through her fingers*


*She felt guilt,*

*She felt sick.*

*She felt a rush to change the world, quick.*

<u>Dark Days</u>

*Our days are numbered in the dark.*

*We are just patiently waiting for someone to turn on the light.*

*Then they'll hold us in their arms and assure us everything will be alright.*

*The darkness that caused so much fright is gone.*

*No more sorrow.*

*No more tears.*

*No more night.*

*All is right.*

<u>Gleam</u>

*The daylight shown a gleam on his face, which made me see him differently.*

*The gleam revealed a smile that had been hidden in the clouds from his past.*

*As he smiled, shock overwhelmed him that he still knew how.*

*But he did.*

*So, he kept on.*

<u>I'm sure</u>


*As I held the door open for you, you quickly passed by without noticing the kind gesture I made towards you.*


*I'm sure your head was still spinning from the narcissistic thoughts turning in your brain, that kept you from thinking of others.*


*And I'm sure that little elderly lady didn't mind that you cut her in line just to buy your almond butter.*


*I'm sure you don't care that you parked in a handicap spot without a sticker or that the man with the false leg had to walk in the rain with his yellow slicker.*


*I'm sure you only care for you and not another. But kindness goes a long way as we help each other.*

<u>Worship</u>

*In the eve we lie awake.*

*Worshipping our bodies*

*In the dark of your room.*

*Your hands rough,*

*Yet gentle enough for my delicate skin.*

*Each freckle, a star to you.*

*My palms lay open wide*

*As I am consumed by you.*

<u>**Blood**</u>

*Blood that covers my hands*

*Drips into a gleaming puddle*

*Creating a river under my feet*

*Causing a mess, it would seem*


*But this blood is cleansing*

*This blood is powerful*

*This blood is life*

<u>**Noisy Brain**</u>

*The noise in my brain*

*Makes its hard for me to sit still*

*And hard for me to retain*


*Absurd thoughts and static are the only frequencies I receive*

*Life's constant uphill battles are difficult for me to perceive*


*Locked in an asylum would be the threat for me*

*If only others saw what I saw in me*

<u>Separate</u>

*Separate lives lead to different people*

*Some threatening, some warm*


*Some will overthrow you the first chance they get*

*The other will embrace you with sweet words and bright eyes*


*Hold onto to them*

*For they are the ones who enrich and fill your life with joy*

<u>Negative Forces</u>

*Your negative forces are always at bay*

*Especially when you speak*

*They try to mold me as clay*


*They twist*

*And they bind*

*To force your opinions*

*As mine*


*But the foundation I stand on*

*Isn't the sinking sand*

*It is on a solid rock that I stand*

www.ingramcontent.com/pod-product-compliance
Lightning Source LLC
Chambersburg PA
CBHW030417160726

47992CB00007B/3165